STANDING IN THE SHADOWS

Bigfoot Stories from Southeastern Ohio

Doug Waller

Otter Bay Books
BALTIMORE, MD 2013

Permission to reproduce in any form
must be secured from the author.

Please direct all correspondence and book orders to:
Doug Waller
465 N. Moose Eye Rd.
Norwich, OH 43767

Library of Congress Control Number 2013936061
ISBN 978-0-615-79270-5

Published for the author by
Otter Bay Books, LLC
3507 Newland Road
Baltimore, MD 21218-2513

www.otter-bay-books.com

Printed in the United States of America

Contents

Acknowledgments

Thanks to my wife Judy for doing without me even when I am home because my mind is usually on Bigfoot. Thanks to all the authors of all the Bigfoot books that I have poured over. Thanks to all the other researchers past and present who have inspired me to pursue this interest I have in Bigfoot. Thanks to Bruce Harrington and others for giving me the opportunity to speak to the public about Bigfoot. Thanks to all of my Facebook friends that I have chatted with and discussed Sasquatch issues with. Thanks to all the gang from SOSBI who have made me proud to have been a founding member of the group. Thanks to Lorena and Mary Lou and all the other witnesses who came forward with their stories of their encounters. Without their cooperation, there wouldn't be a book. Thanks to Mary and my research partner Shawna who remain on the sidelines and whose efforts often go unnoticed but who are an important part of SOSBI. And a very special thanks to Donna Wells Fink for seeing to it that this project got finished. Without her tireless assistance, this venture might never have been completed. Lastly, I would like to give a big thank you to the Bigfoot creatures; for if they had not occasionally crossed paths with the people in this book, the pages herein would be blank. Thank you all.

Introduction

I guess the first recollection I have of Bigfoot that I can remember was from the 1970's when residents of the State of Missouri were seeing some kind of hairy ape-man that was running around their state and terrorizing the local population. Dubbed Mo Mo, short for Missouri Monster, I read about it in newspapers and magazines. One night in a bar after several long necks, I was telling my buddy that I'd like to go out there to Missouri and hunt that thing down with my rifle. Well, good thing it was just beer talk as all I had in my arsenal at the time was a .222 that I hunted groundhogs with. Trying to kill a 7 to 10 foot tall creature that could weigh 1,000 pounds or more with a 50 grain bullet would have been suicide! I remember going to some of Don Keating's Bigfoot meetings in Newcomerstown, Ohio, in the mid 1980's. I never really saw any photos or heard any presentations from the speakers that he would schedule that convinced me that Ohio also had a resident population of Bigfoot. In fact, a lot of what was portrayed as conclusive evidence of Bigfoot's proof of existence did just the opposite for me.

Sometimes at these meetings, members of the audience would tell of sightings and strange occurrences that had happened to them. THAT is what really ignited the flame that I've had for years on this subject. Some of the stories seemed to be pure B.S. but others were so believable with the storyteller making no claims that what he or she saw was definitely a Bigfoot as some of the B.S. talkers had done. The credible witnesses just simply told their story and said that they really didn't know what had made 20 inch tracks in their field or what the 8 foot hairy thing that they saw was. All I had to do was choose to believe them or not. Now I think that anytime you get a room full of people in it, you're going to get a certain percentage of nut jobs. When the subject of the meeting is Bigfoot or UFO's or ghosts or any other thing of this nature, that percentage probably goes way up. But, I still think that some of these people have seen things that can't be explained. I have introduced myself to a number of these people who claim to have had sightings. In fact, I've become friends with some of them and they have convinced me that they are telling the truth. I have also learned that there are people who have had a sighting years ago and didn't tell anyone about it for fear of ridicule. Sometimes a friend or family member will mention Bigfoot years later to them and they will tell them about it if they think they won't be laughed at. Sadly, I'm sure there are some Bigfoot stories that go to the grave with the star witness and are lost forever.

My Search Begins

I didn't really begin searching for Bigfoot evidence in the field until January 2006. I work in a library and from time to time I would see a book about Bigfoot come across the circulation desk. I started reading up on the subject and happened to mention it to Shawna Parks, one of my co-workers, one day and discovered that she, too, was interested in this mystery. When I told her that a local couple whom we both know had a sighting at Salt Fork State Park, Ohio in 2004, she couldn't believe it. We called the couple and asked if we could meet with them and listen to what had happened to them. They did better than that, they agreed to meet with us where the sighting took place and we talked at length about it. These people still go back to the same spot hoping to see one again. Shawna and I decided that we would form a team to look for Bigfoot evidence in the areas around where sightings had taken place. We took our first Bigfoot hunt in January 2006 in Coshocton County, Ohio. Although we didn't find any tracks or other evidence on that trip, we continued to search every 2 or 3 weeks alternating between Coshocton County and Salt Fork State Park areas in Guernsey County. So far, we haven't seen a Bigfoot. We have, on occasion, found tracks. One time we felt we were close to one as we could smell a very strong sulfur smell, which is reported with some sightings. We were way back in the woods in an active known Bigfoot area. The smell was mysteriously absent when we returned through the exact same area 30 minutes later. The area that we hunt in Coshocton County is extremely remote. It is old strip mine land that was never reclaimed and it is a maze of old pits, with a high wall on one side of the lakes and a spoil bank on the other. There are old jeep trails that we walk through. The trail where we smelled the

SOSBI members and researchers, Shawna Parks and Walter Tippie in Salt Fork State Park, Ohio.

sulfur is extremely overgrown in places preventing anyone from driving on it anymore. In some places the brush on either side of the trail forms a tunnel that you have to duck down to get through. Other sections of the trail have standing water and mud where we hope to someday find tracks. It's about a mile back in from where we park the truck to where we smelled the sulfur. We have only smelled it that one time. We have had some return knocks in this area when we have beat on trees with sticks or clubs. It is thought that Bigfoot uses this as a form of communication and researchers have been doing this, too, to try to elicit a response. It was in this same area that I got a spooked feeling one time that was very interesting. Shawna began to whack a tree with a club and got an immediate response from a very brushy area some yards away. I suddenly was overcome with a feeling of extreme uneasiness, not panic or fright mind you. I remember telling Shawna that I wanted to leave, she asked why and I told her, let's go and I'll tell you when we are out of here. About halfway back to the truck I was feeling better and I slowed down my fast pace. I told her that when she hit the tree and we got a return similar sound from the woods, I thought I heard a sound something like a bawl that a cow would make. I then had this feeling of dread and couldn't wait to get out of there. I have since read about other researchers having very similar occurrences happen to them. In his book, *The Locals*, Thom Powell describes an ability called infrasound that he thinks Bigfoot has the capability to use whenever it feels threatened. It produces very low frequency sound waves that human ears can't hear although the human body does receive the signal. It makes the person or persons receiving it very uncomfortable with feelings of anxiety, dread and other unpleasant feelings. You just have to vacate the area. The military is supposed to have experimented with infrasound years ago. The thought was that if they could broadcast these sound waves to the enemy, it would cause the enemy to retreat. You could win a battle without firing a shot. In addition, the ill effects don't last very long, so no one gets hurt. I also believe that Bigfoot has the ability to produce a very strong, unpleasant odor such as a skunk does when it feels threatened or harassed (read page 52 of Lance Orchard's, *The Walla Walla Bigfoot*). Bigfoot, by nature, is timid and not aggressive at all so someone surprising one in the woods could expect the creature to retreat instead of attacking them. Besides producing the bad smell, they also intimidate people by screaming, rock throwing, tree shaking and chest thumping, among other things. I would guess that the creatures don't smell too good to begin with but when needed, if they want to, they can produce a God awful stink that would cause an aggressor to retreat. It's entirely up to the creature to stink the place up or not. I think this is the reason some people report smelling the creature and others don't when they have sightings or close encounters. When Shawna and I smelled the sulfur odor that day, we didn't see a Bigfoot. We did proceed on out the trail very slowly.

When I think back now if we would have just stayed put it's possible it would have screamed, thrown a rock, or fled, giving us a chance to see it. Since we left the area, I believe it stayed put and remained motionless and we didn't see it because of that. In Vance Orchard's book, *Walla Walla Bigfoot*, on page 139, Dr. Ron Brown makes a good point. He says that man is accustomed to hunting for animals that all have a horizontal spine. When you see a deer, elk, rabbit or fox or whatever you're hunting, it will show up among the trees, which are vertical. Because of the animal's spine which is horizontal, it sticks out. We don't hunt any animals with vertical spines like a human's spine. Imagine an upright walking animal that is dark in color in the woods. All it would have to do is stand still by a tree or behind it. It could blend in with the shadows and you wouldn't even know it was there. If you got too close for comfort, meaning it felt threatened, it could then choose to get you to leave by any number of things, big stink, infrasound, screams, rock throwing, etc.

I believe that a Bigfoot's senses would have to be very sharp to have survived as long as they have virtually undetected or officially undiscovered. They are probably well aware of our presence way before we are aware of theirs. Being for the most part nocturnal would help a great deal, as would living in remote areas. Add to that reluctance for witnesses to talk for fear of ridicule and you begin to see why these things are still listed as mythical in most people's minds. Also, don't forget that the majority of scientists will also laugh at the idea of this creature's existence, and most won't even accept the evidence that we do have. They scoff at it as fake, fiction and people's wild imaginations. Some of the evidence I'm sure is faked and that goes a long way to further hamper the creature ever being officially recognized. I believe it was Dr. Grover Krantz who said that science feels this way about Bigfoot, "I'll believe it when I see it," which translates to, I don't believe in it so don't bother me with your plaster casts, hair samples, photographs, or whatever else you have because you're wasting my time. Also, there is tremendous peer pressure among the scientists. Dr. Krantz was ostracized by his colleagues when he stated that he believed the creatures to be real. I'm sure Dr. Jeffrey Meldrum, another scientist, could speak on this very subject, also. So, why is it if these things are as reclusive as it seems that they are, do we occasionally catch a glimpse of them? Well, there are some ways to up your chances of seeing one **if** you want to. First, I would spend a lot of time in areas that have had past sightings. These are not too difficult to locate as the internet has several sites devoted to Bigfoot and locations and dates of sightings are given. I would select an area that has had multiple sightings to begin the search if you are looking for evidence, i.e., tracks, twist-offs, etc. Do your hunting during daylight hours. If you really want to up your chances for a sighting, try your luck at night. Also, I would recommend that you read everything that you can about Bigfoot, Sasquatch, Yeti, etc., and try to learn as much as you can about these creatures. There's lots of information out there on this subject but be cautious of some of it as a lot of it is quite dubious especially on the internet. Some of the internet sites that I personally like are *B.F.R.O.* and Bobbi Short's *Bigfoot Encounters*. Some of the best Bigfoot books that I've read are *The Locals*, by Thom Powell, *Raincoast Sasquatch* by J. Robt. Alley, and anything by John Green, Thomas

Steenburg, Grover Krantz, Loren Coleman, Chris Murphy, Vance Orchard or Mike Quast. Also, check out *Bigfoot Across America*, by Philip Rife and anything pertaining to Bigfoot by Colin and Janet Bord is worth a look. Go to your local library and borrow some books on this subject. If they don't have anything on their shelves they can get it from other libraries, plus it's free as long as it is returned on time. If you read any books that you really enjoy you can buy them from a bookstore or Amazon later on. There are also some videos that offer some insight on Bigfoot. Your local library can help you find these as well.

Another trait that I have learned that Bigfoot possesses is the ability to mimic sounds that other animals make. Why Bigfoot does this is debatable, but I'm sure it must be for a good reason, possibly to make you think it's another animal you hear and not Bigfoot. Another researcher told me about whistling for his dog that was momentarily lost in the woods while on a Bigfoot investigation with him. He would give a distinct whistle and get a near perfect likewise whistle from the woods. Now before you think that some person was whistling back at the man, this was from the woods at 2:00 a.m. in an area that has lots of Bigfoot sightings. Let me continue, in his book *The Locals*, Thom Powell writes about a lady who moved into a farmhouse and lived alone on 170 acres in South Central Virginia. "When I first moved in and tried to go for a walk in the woods taking the pasture road, some huge 'animal' growled and snarled at me from the edge of the woods in the direction I was walking so I immediately returned to the house. That happened several more times when I was in my backyard at the edge of the woods. We did have a small number of bear traffic occasionally but as a rule, they were small brown bears (I think she means black bears, Ursus americanus, as Virginia has no brown bears, Ursus arctos, which live much farther to the north and west of Virginia and not capable of making such large growls.) At any rate I was warned. Next came the daytime hooting of many owls that had a tinge of a man's voice and I decided they must be bootleggers or drug dealers signaling customers for sales. Sometimes they started at 3:00 a.m. and lasted throughout the day. Sometimes they were clearly in my backyard and when they got that close I would sneak out quietly in the dark and shoot over their heads which would take care of the problem for about a month at a time." Another strange thing that happened to her was a strange voice bellowing from the barn in the woods that sounded like someone trying to copy her calling of her little dog Muffin but couldn't exactly get it clear. It was a deep voice, of large capacity. It copied the way she did it. She said that she could understand enough to hear a very rough "Muffin". She also would hear the sound of a front yard full of birds chirping so loudly that they woke her up at 2:00 a.m.

I can't find where I read this to give the author the proper credit but I remember reading somewhere in a book about Bigfoot of a doctor and his wife who lived in a lonely wooded area. He had a long driveway with a locked gate surrounded by woods. They raised chickens and would feed them each day by throwing cracked corn around the yard and driveway. They had seen a Bigfoot around their house, or found its tracks or something, I can't remember exactly, but anyway they knew one was nearby their home. The doctor made sure to always be home and locked inside the house before dark. One fateful day, however, he phoned his wife from the hospital and told her of a terrible traffic accident with many people injured. He would have to work over to tend to these people and he would be home as soon as he could but it would be late. He told his wife to feed the chickens before dark and to lock herself in the house and she would be ok until he got home. Finally, after all the broken bones were set and all the stitches sewn, the doctor was on his way home well after midnight. As he drove along the lonely dark deserted road towards his driveway he kept checking the woods on both sides of the car for any dark shapes or glowing eyes in the tree line (Bigfoot's eyes are supposed to glow red in the darkness). Finally, seeing his driveway up ahead he slowed the car and turned onto the mile long gravel lane that led to his house. When he finally reached the locked gate he could see the lights from the house and felt some relief to be home after such a long day. He could see his wife inside the illuminated house from the car as he exited it to unlock the gate. All he had to do now was swing the gate open, drive through the opening, then shut and lock the gate and go in the house. Just as he was about to unlock the gate, he heard something from the wooded area beside the house. The hair on his arms and neck stood up as he heard a deep voice repeat over and over again, "Chick, chick, chick," as his wife had always done whenever she fed the fowl.

Other sounds that Bigfoot has been credited with making are barking, laughing, screaming, whooping, monkey sounds, squealing, and babies crying. I was surprised to learn that even the Yeti does this. From *My Quest for the Yeti* by Reinhold Messner page 96 and I quote, "A few weeks later a second man, Yang Wanchun, claims to have seen the same hairy man in exactly the same place. Although the Yeti must have noticed him, it came as close as seven or eight feet from Wanchun. A ditch was all that separated them and they stood opposite each other. The hairy human made eleven or twelve different sounds, the chirping of a sparrow, the barking of a dog, the neighing of a pony, the growling of a leopard, the crying of an infant. He made these sounds incessantly for over an hour. So I guess you could say that Bigfoot, Squatch and Yeti are the mocking birds of the mammals."

Another interesting Bigfoot trait is the ability to do things that would require superhuman strength which would, by the way, rule out human hoaxing in many cases. Some of these examples are understandable as to why the creature did them and others leave this researcher scratching his head. For example, the road crew that Jerry Crew was with in Northern California in the late 1950's would return to the work site in the morning to find very large tracks in the dirt, scattered equipment and full 55 gallon fuel drums that had been tossed into a ravine. I think that the creatures were upset to have men invading their home with their loud machines, bulldozers, trucks, etc., so they reacted by trashing the equipment any way they could at night when the men weren't working. This kind of behavior is understandable to me. What I would like an explanation for is why they sometimes do things that would require super strength that may never be seen by anyone unless they just happen to stumble onto it and are puzzled by what they have found. The following are some examples.

Here again my memory fails me and I can't remember what book I read this in but what happened was a man owned some property that had a lane running down through the woods. To keep people from driving down this lane, the man had a gate constructed at the entrance to it. Actually, it was two steel posts set in concrete with a chain stretched between them. The owner could unlock the padlock and drop the chain aside when he wanted access to his property but any other time, the chain was locked up and stretched tight between the two posts. Imagine his surprise when he discovered one morning that someone or something had pulled a concrete anchored post from the ground and laid it aside. No sign of any machinery or tools being used were found at the gate. Only large deep tracks but why didn't the creature simply step over the chain or go around it? Maybe it was leaving a message. Another example, a trapper had a trap set and had it secured by a chain to a very large rock. I can't remember the weight but it was over 75 pounds. It was chained to the rock so the intended quarry wouldn't crawl off with the trap once it was caught. One day the trapper was alarmed to discover that his trap was missing and that happens sometimes when thieves steal things that don't belong to them. But the rock was missing too! The trapper couldn't understand that. Who would steal a big rock? The trap he could understand but this didn't make sense. He searched all around and finally some 100 yards away found his trap still chained to the rock and nothing was in the trap. There was no evidence of the rock having been rolled to its new location, no, it had been carried there, but by who or what? Large tracks were found nearby and the trapper decided that he didn't want to set traps in that area anymore.

Something like this happened to Shawna and me in Coshocton County in 2006. The area that we searched around Plainfield that I spoke of earlier where we smelled the sulfur smell had an old refrigerator that someone had dumped about ¼ mile back in the trail from the township road. We walked right past it two different times when we walked out this trail. We took another couple back there with us and they saw it, too. The next time we went out the trail, maybe a month later, the refrigerator was gone. The thing that puzzles me is who or what took it? The road back into where it was dumped had brush overgrown on both sides of it that almost forms a tunnel in places. We have to duck down to get through on foot. You might get an ATV back in there but not a pickup truck. It would be too large to get through. So, did some men walk back in a quarter of a mile each way and carry out an old junk refrigerator?

I doubt it. Now you may ask how it got there in the first place. Well, years ago you could drive a 4-wheeler back in there, but it's evident by the overgrown brush that it's been years since anyone has. I can't say that a Bigfoot picked up this old abandoned appliance and carried it off because we didn't see it happen, but I can't come up with any other scenario either. Maybe, it's a warning to me not to go back there anymore, or maybe it's telling me to keep out. Probably the most bizarre feat of strength that I have read about is in Robt. Alley's *Raincoast Sasquatch*. He writes of 3 huge cedar trees jammed 30 yards apart into the muskeg in perfectly vertical fashion. This is in an area above Klawock Lake, Prince of Wales Island, Alaska. What is unusual about these trees is that they are upside down with the root wads sticking up in the air. One of them still has the soil clinging to the roots. The largest tree shows 13 feet of wood above the ground, the next largest has 9 feet of wood showing. They estimate that one third of the length of the trees is hidden beneath the ground. According to researcher Al Jackson, they were first reported by his uncle who had told him that he had seen them up there before the logging road went in, in the late 1980's Jackson's uncle had said that he and his buddy, Richmond Benson, would go hunting and fishing with old man, Albert Brown, who died in the early 1960's. Anyway, old Albert would always warn them that whenever hunting above the lake on Klawock Mountain, you have to watch out for those big black gorillas that live up there. He said that they mark their territory by driving blown down trees into the ground, upside down, with the root wads up in the air. Of course, people thought he was making this up until they built the logging roads 40 years later and discovered the trees. He goes on to tell how the trees show no grapple or cable marks from where a helicopter might have dropped them from above. No trace of tread marks in the landscape from any piece of machinery that might have inserted them into the ground inverted in this manner. He says that the largest of the trees probably weighs a thousand pounds and is at a loss to explain how it ended up inserted without any visible marks on its trunk. There are pictures of these trees in his book and they are truly amazing.

Bigfoot/Sasquatch is supposed to be very curious by nature. They are reported to be fascinated by babies and children and the sound of an infant crying or giggling children is apparently enough to draw in some nearby hairy giants for a closer look. Reports have been made of laughing children from a rural school house, during an outside recess that were watched by a tall hairy creature from the adjacent tree line. Another report tells of a family camping with a teething baby. The child became fussy in the night and was crying with discomfort. The father had awoken and was in the process of tending to his child when just then a hairy arm reached in from outside the tent and proceeded to stroke the sobbing child apparently in an attempt to comfort him. Had that father been me, my tent would be posted on e-bay the next day. Another story told of a family that had built a home and had a baby shortly thereafter. The nursery had a video camera in it to record the baby doing whatever it is that babies do. I suspect they had a lot of footage of it sleeping which is what I usually see babies doing. Anyway, the camera was rolling. Little Oswald was in his crib doing his thing and beside the crib was a window. What appeared on the outside looking in through the window watching the sleeping child is what caused the couple to destroy the tape and put their dream home that they had built, up for sale.

"Is That Bigfoot, Mom?"

The curiosity that the creatures have for children is, I believe, responsible for the July 2, 1984 sighting that Lorena Cunningham and her three children had in Noble County, Ohio. Lorena had walked with her kids to a nearby playground so the children could play on the swings, monkey bars, etc. After a few minutes of fun complete with laughter and, "Mom, watch me!" from the youngsters, Lorena heard a sound of brush cracking and something walking in the woods coming closer to the playground. Thinking that it was possibly a cow that had gotten out of a nearby pasture, Lorena walked to the edge of the mowed play area and peered into the woods. Instead of the expected cow, what Lorena saw standing just inside the tree line watching her children play caused waves of terror to shudder through her body. A 7½ foot tall hairy ape-human creature stood just a few yards away from her. She recalled seeing different facial expressions on the creature, curiosity, amusement, even joy, and it showed its teeth but not in a threatening manner, but appeared to almost be smiling as the children continued with their happy sounds they made while playing. Lorena was, at this time, the only one that had seen her (the creature was a female because Lorena mentioned seeing breasts indicating this). She was close enough to see the hair on the creature's head blow in the gentle July breeze. Lorena remembers the color of the creature as being dark with the tips of the hair being red. She was close enough to see the fingernails on its hands. Where the creature's hair was sparse, Lorena could see that the skin was dark. Lorena didn't notice any odor from it nor did she hear it make any sounds other than the sounds of its walking through the brush earlier. The creature's eyes were dark like a cow's eyes she told me, saying it had big dark eyes. It didn't look angry or mean but it was very

Lorena Cunningham's painting of their encounter with the female Bigfoot while she and her children were at the playground in Sharon, Ohio.

intimidating by its sheer size alone. Huge muscles, three to four foot wide shoulders, a very powerful creature was staring at her and her playing children. It looked as though it could kill you in a heartbeat if it wanted to, Lorena told me. Finally, after noticing that their mother was standing frozen in one spot and staring at something in the woods, the two sisters spotted the beast, too, and became frightened and one of the girls ran to Lorena and grabbed her mother's leg in fear knowing that something was terribly wrong and asked her mother, "Is that Bigfoot, Mom?" Lorena answered her that she thinks it is. Her sister, now the only child left on the swings was afraid to come to her mother and finally, after Lorena had summoned up enough courage to call out to her, told her daughter to get off of the swing and walk over to her. Now, with both daughters at her feet and the baby on her hip, she instructed her children to not run, although the natural reaction was to do just that. Lorena instructed her daughters to, "Walk slowly away from it, but keep it in sight if it should come after us." She was afraid that if they ran it would chase them and attack them like a dog or some other unpredictable animal might do. As the troop slowly left the playground and backed up the hill towards their home, Lorena noticed that the hairy creature had disappeared into the woods from which it had earlier appeared. Out of sight but definitely not out of mind, Lorena wondered if it would reappear again and intercept them. Fearing this to be the case, she decided to try to take refuge at her grandmother's house instead of her own as her grandmother's was closer. Lorena remembers seeing her cousin's Doberman Pincher who was tied outside and had also seen the Bigfoot as it watched her kids. The dog was in a state of panic and clawed at the door of the house wanting in. This added to Lorena's terror as the dog had never shown itself to be afraid of anything before. Bigfoot has that effect on dogs and people, too. Other animals, such as cows, horses, deer and even bears are similarly affected. At last safe inside her grandmother's house, Lorena could exhale and try to get her heart rate back down to normal as she tried to calm her frightened children. The oldest daughter is the only child who has any memory of that fateful summer day in 1984 and still refuses to discuss it with anyone, even her own mother! Strange as it may seem, this would only be the first of three encounters Lorena would have with one of these creatures.

It is often said that hindsight is 20/20 and that also proved to be true in this case too as Lorena and her family notified the local authorities of their frightful encounter. Soon, her name got out and people would call the house and make jokes and call her names and do all sorts of mean things to her and her family. Lorena told me that the saddest thing was seeing her daughters run in the house crying after kids on the school bus laughed and said, "Your Momma's crazy!" Lorena's husband also took abuse and remarks from co-workers. She advises

This is the playground where Lorena and her 3 children had their encounter with a female Bigfoot.

against calling the Sheriff's office if you do see one of these things. She said that they told people about her sighting and gave out her name and there were times that she regretted ever having seen it and most definitely reporting it. If one reads enough on the subject of Bigfoot, one will read of this time and time again. Every person that I have ever talked to that had a sighting or other encounter with a Bigfoot has told me this. Some people after a while clam up and will not talk about it anymore even to friends or family members. Lorena did have a few allies though. An elderly farmer told her that he believed her as he had seen it three different times while he fed his cattle. It would stand at the tree line and silently watch him as he did his chores. The farmer stated that it never bothered him so he never bothered it. No mention was made however of how far away it was or what his cattle thought of the whole thing. The man has since passed on so no further info is available from him. Another neighbor reported to her that something had knocked down her birdfeeder one night during the winter. Suspecting deer or raccoons, the lady was surprised to find huge human-like barefoot tracks in the snow that pointed a biased finger towards our furry friend, Bigfoot.

Another incident involved a young man who, during bow season, hung a tree stand in the nearby woods with thoughts of filling his freezer with venison and maybe putting a trophy buck mount on his wall. All thoughts of the above were scrapped when a Bigfoot walked under it while our friend, the bow hunter, sat transfixed unable to believe his eyes. I asked Lorena if there was any chance of my talking with this guy and she said no because he took his stand down and never came back again and refuses to discuss it with anyone now.

Lorena with Natalie, a producer with the Finding Bigfoot show, holding Lorena's sculpture of the female Bigfoot she witnessed with her children at the playground.

Lorena also had an experience with a Bigfoot inside a barn that would curl the hair on a bald man or at least make it stand up. The story goes like this, one day Lorena was asked by her daughter to feed the horses for her, that she kept at Lorena's father's farm, because she wanted to go someplace and she wouldn't be home in time to do it. It was only a few minutes after entering the structure that Lorena realized that something was amiss. The horses wouldn't come into the barn to feed and this was in January and they seemed afraid of something inside the barn. None of the barn cats were around either which was highly unusual. As Lorena filled the stalls with hay, the eerie silence was finally broken with a muffled thump and sudden realization that she wasn't alone in the barn! What thoughts must have raced through her mind when she realized that something was above her in the hayloft and its massive weight caused the floor boards to creak and sag above her head? She felt the hair on her arms and the back of her neck raise. Bits of hay fluttered down between the cracks of the floor whenever it moved. So, this is why the horses won't come into the barn to eat she thought. It also explains the absence of any of the barn cats that were always underfoot waiting for a handout. She thought of her

This is a painting done by Lorena Cunningham of her encounter with a Bigfoot above her in the loft of her father's barn.

children and that day at the playground 20 years before when that "thing" had appeared out of the trees. "God help me. Will I live to ever see my kids again?" she prayed. Lorena gripped the pitchfork she'd been using tighter now and even armed herself with a second one just in case the huge beast should decide to descend the ladder and confront her. She remembered thinking that she refused to go down without a fight. She tried to catch a glimpse of the creature through one of the many cracks in the floor over her head, wanting to confirm what she suspected was moving about above her while at the same time praying that she didn't see it. Finally, the sagging of the floor above her moved to the far end of the hayloft, giving her the chance for escape out the small barn door in the opposite direction as she latched it behind her. When her daughter and her fiancé returned to the farm, they noticed that the small barn door was standing open. They thanked Lorena for feeding the horses, but told her that she had left the small barn door open. When Lorena explained to them what had occurred, her daughter was not too surprised. This was Lorena's older daughter who clearly remembered the day when she was young and the female Bigfoot was watching them on the playground. She also refused to speak of the Bigfoot and would become frightened and hide under the kitchen table whenever anyone talked of it when she was younger. Lorena's younger daughter and son remembered nothing of the Bigfoot from that day. This daughter now told her mother that she had recently been hearing grunts and noises like monkeys would make somewhere behind the barn but hadn't told anyone. This property has since been sold and the barn is gone now.

This is Lorena's father's barn where the Bigfoot was in the hayloft overhead.

In the picture above, inside Lorena's father's barn,
the overhead hayloft is on the right
and on the left is the lower level where Lorena stood.

Here Lorena surveys the area of the barn near the grain bin.
I noticed that when taking pictures in this area,
white orbs are usually seen.

The Bigfoot Diary

I met and became friends with the Ringer's, Don and Mary Lou, who resided in a beautiful old 2-story house that Mary Lou's family had built in the late 1800's. Their home is situated in the center of Guernsey County's Knox Township. The farm consisted of well over 100 acres of pastures, fields and woods with deep ravines and rock outcroppings. These rocky areas are abundant in Southeastern Ohio. When the glaciers melted and slid south thousands of years ago, it scraped flat most of the Buckeye State but stopped short of this area. Instead of being flat, this area consists of hills and valleys with deep gorges and huge boulders jutting out of the hillside. To look at some of this terrain one almost can imagine Native Americans hiding among the many crevices waiting to attack any unsuspecting white men foolish enough to venture into their territory. With that being said, it's not hard to imagine a shy reclusive creature also inhabiting these areas as there are plenty of places to hide. It's also difficult to walk in some of these steep hollows so few people ever go. After befriending Don and Mary Lou, I was invited to their home for a visit. With my wife Judy and Shawna in tow, we drove out the lonely country roads of Knox Township until we came to their home. We were invited in and given a tour of the downstairs of the dwelling and after a brief history of the house we were asked to sit in the parlor while Don retrieved his *Bigfoot Diary*. We sat spellbound for several minutes as Don read from his notes and retold stories of hearing screams, tree knocks, track finds, frightened cattle and a host of other odd and eerie happenings that had occurred in the past 20 years on their property with everyone now in a rather anxious mood. We were next ushered into the dining room for peach cobbler and coffee. By this time, it had become quite dark outside and as I sat in the

This is the Ringer's barn.

candlelit room after hearing of all the Bigfoot activity that this property has had I was almost expecting to see one peeking in the window at us as we enjoyed our dessert. As I was to find out later in several of the books about Bigfoot that I've read, curiosity is one of their traits. More than one unsuspecting person has looked up from their book or TV screen or whatever to see a Bigfoot on the outside looking in at them. This was rather unnerving to learn and it's caused us to usually lower the curtains after dark in our own home just in case we should be visited by such a curious giant in the night.

Bigfoot Diary

Oct 85	We moved to country
Jan 89	ML saw footprint in snow behind wagon shed
Summer 92	night after night – screams in woods north of house
Winter 93-94	Very cold winter – cattle afraid to go into barn
Summer 94	heard tremendous scream in woods south of house one evening at dusk – date unknown
Aug 19-94	approx 9:30 – wood on wood
Aug 24-94	ditto
Aug -94	Sunday evening about 9:30 ML in town – scream in driveway beside house – bad window fan on
Feb 99	after dark – 3 strikes wood on wood south of house
Feb 1-99	1:45 – heard two calls – not screams – one close to house below barn, and about 45 seconds later another one further away as if creature walking
July 2004	about 7:00 AM – 3 strikes on front porch – then here – going and headed toward barn striking things
Apple tree stripped Fall of '06	
Fall '06	ML heard tree knocking in woods in most or Nov

This is a picture of Don Ringer's Bigfoot Diary that he wanted the author to have. Included with the diary was a file full of Don's notes and newspaper clippings of Bigfoot sightings.

I have had some near misses with Bigfoot. By near misses, I mean being at the wrong place at the wrong time or even the right place too early or too late. Let me explain. On January 27, 2007, Shawna and I went to Noble County to check for any Bigfoot evidence that may have been present in that county. A new snow was on the ground and we hoped we might get lucky and find some tracks. However, nothing unusual was found. Later that evening as I was lounging around at home, Judy and I got a phone call from Mary Lou Ringer. She was very excited and asked to speak with me after talking with Judy for a few minutes. I remember being uncomfortable at first, talking to her as her husband Don had just died. In fact, this very day, January 27, 2007, was the day of his funeral. Maybe I felt a little guilty that we hadn't attended the service. We had sent a card as I remember. Anyway, as I took the phone from Judy and gave condolences to Mrs. Ringer, she quickly thanked me and then announced, "It was back!" I fired back at her, "What or who was back?" "Bigfoot!" she answered. She said that she had tracks in her yard in the snow. I said that I would come right over. I told her that it's starting to spit a little rain here as it's warmed up a little bit outside and that she had better put a cardboard box or something over some of the tracks to protect them from the rain. I quickly grabbed my camera, flashlight and a few other things and was on my way to her house in a matter of minutes. Judy went with me on this trip and she was very nervous at the thought of maybe seeing a Bigfoot at close range at night. We pulled into Mary Lou's driveway at 8:20 p.m. I had seen 3 deer in a field across the road from her house. Also, the cattle were all standing around by the barn. None of the animals seemed to be upset or afraid so I took this to mean the creature was no longer anywhere around the house or barn. After exiting the truck, I met Mary Lou at the back door and she related to us the story of these tracks in her yard. She and her brother, Paul, who was there with her when we arrived, had gone to the funeral service in the late morning that day and as I said earlier there was snow on the ground. People had driven in and out of the driveway several times that day to drop off food and such at her house. The sidewalk from the driveway leading up to the back door was swept clear of snow. When she and Paul returned home, which I believe she said was around 6:30 or 7:00 p.m., she saw the tracks in her yard and recognized them as being the same or similar to the ones she had seen years ago coming out of the barn. She told me that they were not there earlier in the day when they left the house to go into town. Paul got a crash course in Bigfoot as she had never mentioned anything to him ever about the creature and all the experiences she and Don had had over the years at their home. Paul held the light for me and asked what we were looking for while I measured the track length at 20" and the stride at 62". I tried to explain to him what it was that had left these huge tracks in the yard and the possible size of the beast that put them there. He took it all in stride and seemed to enjoy this bit of investigative work and asked several more questions. He never once showed any signs of being afraid or wanting to go back inside the house. I was impressed by this 82 year old man that night and continue to be so as I have seen other men, and I use this term loosely, who are afraid of being anywhere around where Bigfoot has been while claiming to be a researcher in this field. I tried to duplicate the stride of the tracks in the snow and was unable to do so. I'm 6'2" so it had to be much taller than me. The tracks had the trademark of one directly in front of the other that these creatures seem to always leave. If you have seen pictures in books you will know what I mean by this. I got 3 or 4 good photos of this long stride exiting the back door area and going across the yard only to be lost in the jumble of the many tire tracks in her driveway. The thing that gets me is the direction of the tracks. They are walking away from the back of the house. No tracks were found going in the direction to the house. It had to have walked up to the back door of the house on the sidewalk that was swept free of snow. Then for some reason it left the house not by the same clean sidewalk but by going right through virgin snow in the yard leaving behind these mammoth imprints for Mary Lou to discover. And to have paid a visit to this home on the very day of the resident's funeral! It's almost as if it knew of Don's passing and was somehow paying its respect. We found some more of the oversized footprints on the other side of the driveway going to and from a fence where the pasture begins. These prints show the toes very well in the photos. The creature took short choppy steps here as the ground is not level and having been snow covered it would have been easy to slip and fall. I didn't find any other tracks around the house that night and after looking at the pictures, I tried to piece together how the shaggy leviathan had entered the yard. I have concluded that he came in from the south out of the deep woods and below the barn to the fence by the stone house. Here is where he stepped over the fence by the stone house and proceeded up to the house, for whatever reason we'll probably never be sure. He left the same way. That tells me he wasn't just passing through. No, he was there for a reason, I believe. I just don't know for sure yet what it was. . .

Did the Bigfoot visit to pay his respects to Don? Here are the tracks in the snow as the Bigfoot left the Ringer's home the day of Mr. Ringer's funeral. Starting in about the middle of the picture the Bigfoot trail leading away from the house can clearly be seen.

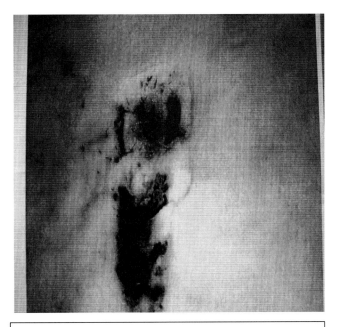

*Footprints in the snow leading away from the
Ringer's home the day of Don's funeral.*

One morning at work before we'd opened for business I heard a knock at the front door. Thinking maybe one of the other co-workers had lost their keys I responded to the noise and was surprised to find Mary Lou Ringer at the door. "I have to tell you what happened last night," she whispered. I stepped outside and listened as she told me of being awakened out of a sound sleep at 3:30 a.m. "It was a tremendous scream that seemed so loud that it could not have been from anything human," she told me. She said that the scream had to have come from something very large and very close to the house. Looking out of the second story window from the bedroom didn't reveal what or exactly where this rude awakening had come from. Summoning monumental amounts of courage for anyone, let

33

alone a female senior citizen, Mary Lou descended the stairs and went to the front door and looked outside as she prayed that the nocturnal intruder wasn't inches from the door when she pulled it towards her. Another scream shattered the darkness and she quickly closed the door and locked it! With her heart racing like a train, she hurried to the kitchen to confirm that the back door was locked, too. Although, she thought, what good would a flimsy little lock do to keep out something of the size that this thing had to be in order to be able to make a scream of that volume? What good would the door do for that matter if it really wanted in, if it would even fit through the door that is? No, she told herself. Don't think that way. These things are not supposed to be violent. Doug had assured her that she was not in any danger of being attacked by these creatures! After all, hadn't she and her late husband lived in this very house for over 20 years with these giants coming around every so often and screaming or hitting trees or even the house but they had never tried to get in! Another scream broke the silence and she could tell from the kitchen that her first guess was right. It was north of the house and across the road from the front yard. It let out another wail and that was answered by a similar sound but further away. She again heard the one closest to the house but it sounded like it had changed its position and was moving towards the other one further off. Its next scream confirmed this. It was leaving to join the other one further away. With trembling fingers she made a pot of coffee and sat at the kitchen table. She strained to listen for another scream but none came. She poured herself a cup of coffee and looked at the kitchen clock. It was 4:15 a.m. and it had been 15 minutes since she last heard any sound from the outside. Had it really left? She hoped so. But she couldn't go back to bed. I don't want to be awakened by a scream like that ever again, she thought. More coffee, more clock watching, it was a long night for Mrs. Ringer. It was well after 5:00 a.m. when fatigue overpowered fear and the caffeine that was in her system and Mary Lou climbed the stairs and collapsed into bed.

After Don passed away, Mary Lou gave me a gift of Don's *Bigfoot Diary* saying she knew Don would have wanted me to have it. I felt very honored to be the new keeper of his diary.

One of the stories in Don's *Bigfoot Diary* concerned 2 hunters and their Bigfoot encounter as they hunted on the Ringer's property in the early 1980's. I met with the hunters at Mrs. Ringer's to talk about what had occurred. As I sat across the table from them and listened as they recounted their story from some twenty-five years ago, I couldn't help but think about my own deer hunting past. My first whitetail deer, a doe, was shot no more than a mile from where we sat now. It could have been the same year (1983) as the story that the men told. They could only guess at the year. But both men agreed that it was in the early 1980's. The night before opening day of deer gun season has always been known as a night of very little sleep for hunters. Visions of the big buck always seem to prevent them from getting the rest that they need. So come Monday morning, armies of orange clad gunners take to the field operating on pure adrenaline and maybe some caffeine, too, for good measure. But what kept these men awake was different. It wasn't the usual worries of whether or not the hunters brought enough cold weather gear, and their rain suits, and their knives, or a thousand other things that keep men awake at night. No, what kept Roger Peterson and Don Wissmar awake that night was fear. It was the fear of what was out there and fear of the unknown. When they first heard the scream, they said they looked at each other and both thought of where they had heard that sound before. It sounded a lot like elk when they bugle, but yet different. This sound reverberated up from the valley below to the small encampment, that of a pop-up camper, van and a pick-up truck the men had parked there only hours before. Summoning their three hunting companions from the camper the quintet strained to hear the sound again just to be sure that they hadn't imagined it. Now, with only the sound of their own heartbeats and the crackling of their campfire, all other sounds were absent as if every living thing on this property had vanished or retreated while this deafening screaming of whatever it was transgressed on the very same ground that the men had planned to hunt on the very next day. Whatever it was it was very loud and very fast Roger told me. That particular tract of land where this happened consists of 117 acres and stretches down to the neighbor's fence some 2000 feet below. The men said that as the creature screamed and raced back and forth, they estimated that it traveled the length of this particular hollow in less than 5 minutes. After some 6 or 8 screams that would raise or lower in volume, depending on if the creature was coming towards them or going away from them, all became quiet, very quiet, not one sound, from anywhere. It had gone away. But it had let them know that it wasn't happy that they had set up camp on what it apparently considered its domain. Our hunters finally retreated back into their sleeping bags, 3 in the camper, Roger and Don in the pickup and van. They settled down for a few hours of restless slumber. Visions of huge wide racked bucks brought smiles to their sleeping faces like little children on Christmas Eve. Yeah, right, not this night and not the next night either, or any others for a long, long time, until what happened that night faded from their memories a bit.

The Pony

   Our next fellow who had a brief but startling
introduction to Bigfoot I've decided to call Norman Andrews as
he wishes to remain anonymous. You see Norman had a pony
for his kid to ride. The pony, being quite cantankerous as some
ponies are prone to be, wouldn't stay in his fenced enclosure
where he was supposed to be. He was always tearing the fence
down and getting out. Norman would catch the pony, repair the
fence and all was well until the next time he escaped, which he
did quite often. Finally, Norman tired of this and had to sell the
little steed. End of story, right? Well, not quite, because one day
sometime afterward, Norman was looking for something in the
shed and discovered that he still had some 50 or 60 pounds of
feed for the now departed little fellow. Norman wondered what
he was going to do with the pony feed. He decided to dump the
remaining feed on the ground behind the shed. The deer might
as well have it he thought so he dumped 50 pounds of feed into a
big pile on the ground. Now, this being in Guernsey County and
only a few miles south of the Salt Fork dam, it shouldn't have
taken the numerous deer in the area too long to discover this
wonderful bounty. But the deer never got the chance to find the
feed because something else found it first, something tall, black
and hairy. Now that I have your full attention, let me tell you the
whole story as Norman told it to me. This took place in early
March 2008 around 9:00 p.m. Norman went outside to feed the
rabbit which was in a pen behind the house and shed where they
kept its food. "The rabbit was really spooked about something.
He was in the closed box part of his pen and wouldn't come out
when I put the food in the cage," Norman began. The rabbit had
never done this before and Norman remembered thinking how
strange that was. The rabbit must have seen what devoured the

whole 50 pounds of horse feed that night because it was only about 50 feet beyond the rabbit pen and it was all gone the next day Norman discovered the next morning. After Norman closed the door of the cage, he proceeded back towards the house. Wanting to go visit his father-in-law, Norman walked down the driveway towards the man's trailer some 50 yards away. As he walked, he could hear someone or something walking parallel to him in the woods. There is a wooded hill behind his house that had an old roadbed running parallel to the driveway. Thinking maybe it was a deer, Norman would stop and listen and each time Norman stopped, it would stop, too. A deer wouldn't do that he thought to himself. Proceeding on a little further, he came to a place where the trees and multiflora rose wasn't quite as thick as before and so he stopped again and squinted his eyes and tried to see what was following him some 30 feet to his right. Now Norman was sure that he could make out some dark figure on the path beside him and he was positive that it was not on 4 legs but 2. Walking faster now, Norman reached the porch of the old man's trailer and was reaching for the door when all of a sudden his walking companion, who by now was out ahead of him, triggered a motion detector, activated a floodlight and was fully illuminated by not one but 2 of GE's finest 150 watt floodlights. The startled giant let out a scream that stood Norman's neck hair on end and lengthened its stride to greater proportions. It walked past a parked pickup truck in its hast to leave and towered over the cab of the truck much like Manute Bol towered over Spud Webb whenever their paths crossed. Norman remembers smelling a very powerful wet dog smell about this time that saturated the air in the immediate area. "It didn't break into a run; it just walked up the hill and out of sight." With those enormous strides, it was gone in 3 seconds after that light came on. When I interviewed Norman for this book, I asked him if any neighboring dogs were barking that night. Norman said he didn't remember but that one of his cats was spooked earlier that evening and scratched at the door until the cats were let inside. Then they hid. I wonder if the pony wasn't spooked all along because the Bigfoot was watching it from up above on the hill. Oh, and one more thing about this report, Norman now feeds the rabbit before dark!

Norman was standing here on his father-in-law's porch when the motion sensor turned the lights on and he saw the Bigfoot step over the wood pile in the center of the photo and walk past the trucks and up the road where it threw back its head and screamed.

Broadhead Road Sighting

The only thing Doris had on her mind at the time was what to take out of the freezer for dinner that night as she piloted her black Jeep Liberty up Broadhead Road. This being mid-November with the deer in the midst of breeding season 8:30 at night combined with the fact that she was traveling uphill on the washboard road that this section of Broadhead is, she was only going about 30 mph. Suddenly, the brown/grey roadbed that her headlights illuminated disappeared into total black then reappeared to its original brown/grey color. Only then did she realize that something had passed in front of her as she her car climbed the hill. Turning her head to the left revealed the source of the momentary eclipse. Standing not 20 feet away was a tall, dark creature, not of the handsome kind mind you, but the kind that most people refuse to believe even exists! The Jeep had coasted to almost a standstill at the time and in the few seconds that it took for Doris' brain to digest all the information that her wide open eyes were sending it, she mashed the gas pedal. She began a furious slapping and pummeling of the inside door panel of the Jeep in the area around the lock the likes of which hadn't been seen since the Rodney King beating in 1991. Her desperate attempt at security finally came when she located the lock button and slammed it down. She recounted to me that it was only then that she saw that the creature had stopped by a tree on the left side of the road and had placed one of its hands on the tree to steady itself before it slid down the bank. She said that she definitely saw fingers on the hand. It was not a paw. It was a hand with fingers. In an instant it was gone, down the bank and into the darkness wherever it was headed. Doris too, continued on her way but at a much faster speed than before all the while her eyes searching the road ahead and beside of her. Her heart, pounding like a drum, along with her eyes which had seen it was now convincing her brain that what she had just witnessed was indeed for real and not just a myth!

SOSBI Is Born

After having attended numerous Bigfoot meetings in the surrounding area for a couple of years, Shawna and I always came away from them wanting more. By this time, we had met others who shared an interest in the subject and we decided to hold some meetings of our own and so we did with splendid results. We all sat around on my screened porch (it was the largest room we could get for free) in a circular arrangement and talked Bigfoot. There was no guest speaker, no schedule, no agenda, just 12 to 15 people discussing, asking and answering questions about Bigfoot. We always included refreshments and enjoyed a very casual atmosphere where people could ask and tell all of their thoughts and questions about what these hairy giants actually were and how in the world they have lived among us humans for all this time virtually undetected. It became evident after 3 or 4 of these meetings that we were going to have to find a larger room to hold them in as we had to be careful and not invite more than what my porch would hold. We sure didn't want to overload the structure and cause it to collapse. I could see the headline now, *Porch Collapse Sends Bigfoot Believers to Hospital*. By this time, in the fall of 2008, we asked a co-worker, Mary, to go to one of the other Bigfoot meetings in the area with us and while in attendance, I ran into Chris Furry, an acquaintance from my high school days who was in the audience. He shared with us a couple of Bigfoot incidents that he had experienced and we began plans to start holding public meetings on the subject with the four of us conducting them. We asked the library director where I work and he requested permission at the library board meeting for us to use the meeting room in the library and we were granted use. We had discussed what we would call our group beforehand and with many trials and suggestions, we settled on the Southeastern Ohio Society for Bigfoot Investigations or SOSBI for short. The first meeting was held at the Byesville Branch Library in November 2008. We had 25 people in attendance. It became clear very quickly after only one meeting we would need to find a bigger room as 25 in the meeting room of the Byesville Library is a full house. We then scheduled another meeting for two months later to be held at the recently constructed Crossroads Branch Library in Cambridge. We continue to this day to meet every other month at Crossroads with large crowds attending (on one occasion, we had 73 people in attendance) with no program planned and no speakers. We invited just Bigfoot minded people showing up to talk about their favorite subject. Our audience consists of Bigfoot researchers, investigators, witnesses, people who are just curious or interested in Bigfoot and sometimes even a skeptic or two. I start the meetings by explaining how the open forum works and telling the crowd that I will act as the moderator. After making an announcement or two, I ask if anyone has anything they want to discuss or ask about. Sometimes it takes a while for the new people to open up and tell of their experiences with Bigfoot. Often, after we have taken a break for refreshments, they feel more at ease and without too much coaxing, they tell what happened to them. The others are given time to ask them questions and take notes and discuss their event at length. We encourage the audience to meet and exchange names and phone numbers. We provide a venue for them to talk about their sighting to others without fear of ridicule. Actually, we are a support group for some witnesses who have been made fun of sometimes for years by friends and even family members. Some of our regulars have become close friends with others at the meetings. We also have investigators/researchers attend our meetings who meet and talk to each other and the witnesses and plan excursions and campouts in Squatchy areas and then report their findings at the meeting. This gives everyone the opportunity to show their pictures or videos to the group. Sometimes one will bring in a plaster cast of a Bigfoot track to show everybody. Occasionally the talk wanders off of Bigfoot and strays over to some other oddity such as UFO's, orbs, or ghosts and it's my job as moderator to steer them back to Sasquatch. Some of this other stuff is quite interesting and a few times when there hadn't been any new reports on Bigfoot I let them go on about the UFO's since quite a few of the Bigfoot sightings that I have read about contain UFO sightings taking place in the same vicinity at the same time as the Sasquatch sightings. Stan Gordon, a researcher from Pennsylvania, has a book out called *Silent Invasion* that is full of sightings of both and sometimes occurring together.

Doug Waller leads the SOSBI Southeastern Ohio Society for Bigfoot Investigation meeting at the Crossroads Library in Cambridge, OH in March 2013.

Bigfoot on display at the Cambridge, Ohio library.

I took a Guernsey County map and mounted it on a cardboard stand. It shows all of the different townships each in a different color and of course, all the roads, rivers, lakes and streams, etc. Then I started to assemble as many Bigfoot sightings, track findings, tree breaks, etc., that took place in Guernsey County. It is something that has data added to it often and it's a hands-on reference piece that is very popular with most people especially older folks who aren't computer trained. It has a guide that is written on the side that explains what the different colored pins stuck in it mean to the observer. Yellow pins mean a sighting, orange means tracks were found, blue means vocalizations were heard, etc.

*This is the group camping area where SOSBI holds
its meetings during the warmer months.*

We have had some strange things happen during SOSBI events that I can't explain and I am aware of similar things happening to others in other states. An example is the strange lights of Salt Fork during the fall of 2012. We had a combination meeting/campout at the group camping area of Salt Fork. This is a great area to camp and research in. It's easy to get to, it's off by itself, it's only $5 to camp, and the group rate is $5 per person per night. We sometimes have the whole campgrounds to ourselves. Plus, there have been sightings in and around the campground in the past. On this particular event, one of our campers, Michelle, got up at 4:30 a.m. to use the outhouse and she heard a scream emitting from the nearby woods followed by coyotes howling and carrying on. She was taking video with her phone to get the audio saved to playback for the other campers who were still asleep. Just as she stopped recording the video (you couldn't really see anything in the video, just darkness at 4:30 a.m. but you could hear the howling) she snapped a picture in the direction of the howling in the darkness. What she got when she checked her phone later surprised her as well as everyone else who examined it. It shows the darkened campground in the foreground with a bush in the center of the photo. You can make out the corner of one of the two outhouses with trees to the left, the right and straight ahead, maybe 40 yards ahead which is where she said the howling seemed to be coming from. What the picture shows is baffling. In the photo there appears to be an extremely bright light shining down from above as if a helicopter was hovering above the campground with a powerful searchlight on it.

Michelle says that she heard absolutely no noise whatsoever except for the howling coyotes and there was no light as this was 4:30 a.m. and that rules out any sun or sunrise. Yet, there is a light shining down from above as if it was high noon. What makes this even more bizarre is Michelle didn't see the light with her own eyes and neither did her father whom she had woken up when she first heard the scream. She can faintly be heard talking in the video she took before she snapped the picture. I asked her what she took a picture of in the first place if she couldn't see the light. She answered that she was hoping to get a picture of the screaming, howling coyotes that were directly in front of her in the trees ahead. When word got out to the other campers, one of them told of seeing strange lights in the woods on Friday night, which was the night before. He and another camper were sitting over at the handicapped picnic area in the wee hours of the morning listening for screams or wood knocks when they begin to see strange light balls near the ground coming from the woods on the road into the pavilion at the Bigfoot hotspot in the park. The men got in their car and tried to chase down the source of the lights and were unable to do so. All they reported was that there was a State Trooper driving around inside the park that followed them nearly all the way back to the Parker Road Group Camping area where all of us were staying. Was this the same light that Michelle saw the next night? The men could see the lights. Michelle couldn't see hers, but it was in her picture. They didn't get a picture of their lights; they all said that there was no noise coming from the lights. What were they? I have no idea.

This is Michelle's picture taken in complete darkness at 4:30 a.m. at the campground at Salt Fork State Park. There appears to be a light shining down on the area that wasn't seen when Michelle took this picture.

SOSBI holds a meeting during one of its campouts at Salt Fork State Park.

Bigfoot and the UFO Connection?

A similar event happened to Jackie and Donna, Wisconsin Bigfoot researchers, in May of 2012 in Southern Wisconsin. The girls were out on a Saturday night doing Bigfoot research in an area where many strange things have been reported by the duo. The pair have found tracks, some are Bigfoot suspected, others seem to be extra-large wolf-like prints (walking on 2 legs) and others seem to be huge cougar prints and in an area too far south and not known to have wolves, cougars or even bears. Witnesses who live close-by have reported to the team that they have seen Bigfoot, Dogmen, UFO's and a host of other cryptids. Sounds similar to Salt Fork, doesn't it? Donna and Jackie have seen UFO's there on several occasions and the first time was the night before Easter 2012. These researchers were sitting in a truck preparing to get out and look around for Bigfoot. It was exactly 9:57 p.m. when the girls noticed a round white light flying into their area from far off in the northwest skies. As the light drew closer, the girls wondered aloud if it was a plane flying too low coming at them or a helicopter or maybe an ultra-light plane, Donna says she suggested in a moment of desperation. Jackie says she told Donna that ultra-lights don't fly at night and don't have lights on them. Suddenly, they said, they saw that the round white light had stopped and was hovering silently about 50 feet off the ground and about 160 yards directly across the empty cornfield from them. It was hovering right next to the woods where the Bigfoot was witnessed for a second time in late summer of 2011. Donna says Jackie started frantically tearing at the coats and extra layers of clothing in the truck that they had brought along to wear and she asked Jackie what she was doing. Jackie said, "We have to hide. We have to hide. Start the truck and let's get out of here."

Donna said that in spite of being very frightened herself, she thought it was extremely funny that Jackie thought she could hide under coats and sweatshirts and the aliens wouldn't know they were there. Donna told her she wasn't going to start the truck and drive away because that would turn on the truck lights and the aliens might follow them home. So, they sat there in terror and disbelief for over 45 minutes while the UFO changed shapes and colors, blinked on and blinked off and then finally flew further away from them and hovered for about 15 minutes over the duck pond and then the UFO seemed to fly further away over the marshes and hovered there for approximately 15 minutes and then couldn't be seen any longer. The girls said that because of Jackie's job, they could only go and look for the UFO and Bigfoot on Saturday nights. But every Saturday night for the next 5 weeks, at approximately the same time, the UFO would fly in from the same part of the sky and on these subsequent visits it would hover farther away over the duck pond which was too far away for them to photograph with their cameras. The girls said they wished they had had the courage to get out of the truck and photograph the UFO the first time they saw it because that was the closest to them they would ever see it again. They were so scared of being abducted the first time they saw the UFO that Jackie even rolled down the window and crawled out because she had to go to the bathroom so badly and then she crawled right back in the window the same way she went out! The girls even drove around the road to the back of the pond but by the time they arrived, the UFO could no longer be seen. They don't know whether it left or if it had just blinked out for a time. The duo said they even tried to follow the UFO one time as it flew farther away. They were able to keep it in their view for a few miles but they finally saw it change into just two red orbs and then they lost sight of it on the winding roads. So, on the sixth consecutive Saturday night of going out to see the UFO, the girls and their friend, Leah Ann, actually set up lawn chairs on a huge swath of grass close to the marshy grasses that led to the woods that circled the duck pond in the hopes of seeing the UFO more closely and maybe even finally getting a good picture. The UFO had never bothered them, so the girls became much braver with each sighting. It was a beautiful night and they could see the moon over their left shoulders shining brightly over the woods where Bigfoot had been seen. Leah Ann even took a picture of the moon over the Bigfoot woods that evening. As the girls waited and waited for the UFO to show up, they became more and more disappointed that here they were close enough to get a good picture and this would be the first time in six consecutive Saturday nights that the UFO didn't come. Just goofing around because they were getting bored waiting for something to happen, Donna took a picture of the woods surrounding the duck pond and the sky above. There was nothing in the woods or the sky, Donna thought, when she took that picture. However, about a month later, Donna attended her high school reunion and took a lot of pictures. Upon reviewing the photos that she had taken she happened upon the picture she had taken of the woods surrounding the duck pond and the sky above. She was shocked to see in the picture that in the sky above the woods was a brightly lit white UFO shaped like barbells and looking more closely at the photo, she saw 2 red orbs in the woods below. Donna said that at first she was scared at the photo she saw and barely slept that night but upon waking in the morning felt a sense of amusement at the picture. She said she felt she had received a gift of a photo from whoever has been visiting their Bigfoot area in their silent airship but also like she and Jackie were part of an inside joke with the beings. Now, the UFO still comes hovering in the sky sometimes when they are out after dark and looking for Bigfoot and it still changes shapes and colors, blinking out and back on, but never close enough to actually photograph with their point and shoot cameras. Although, as this book was being typed, Donna said she just saw the UFO come sailing into their area this past Saturday night while they were in the Bigfoot woods. She said she yelled twice for Jackie to come out of the woods and look because the UFO was back, but by the time Jackie crawled out of the Bigfoot shelter, the UFO went hazy and then blinked out completely. They are sure it was still there, just invisible.

This is the picture taken by Donna Wells Fink & Jackie Riesterer of the SWWO Southern Wisconsin's Wild Ones. At the time the picture was taken, there was nothing visible in the sky above these woods. The moon was over their left shoulders. This UFO has been seen hovering silently in the areas of where a Bigfoot has been sighted on numerous occasions. Notice also the 2 orbs in the woods.

Coshocton County

Tyler dreamed of taking a big buck with his crossbow. He had checked the ODNR brochures and found that the biggest bucks and the most deer taken in Ohio were killed in the region of the state starting with Knox and Licking counties and traveling east into Coshocton, Muskingum, Tuscarawas and Guernsey counties continuing eastward towards the Ohio River. Tyler was especially intrigued with Coshocton County. This area led the state in deer kills in 2011 with close to 8000 deer taken, four or five times more than his home county of Butler. He had researched it on line and found that Coshocton County has a good amount of public land to hunt on too which was a blessing for he only had one other place to hunt and it hadn't been very productive lately with very few deer being seen. Coshocton County offers the Woodbury Wildlife area, the AEP Coal Company lands and the Muskingum Watershed District Wills Creek area. He needed an area that provided public hunting but not too public, he didn't feel comfortable with very many other hunters in the area. He needed a place where he could get way back in and still be on public land yet be relatively all alone. He came up with a plan to put himself in one of the best deer counties in the State of Ohio and yet have it pretty much to himself. It all sounded pretty good on paper but as someone once said about football games, they're not played on paper. Translation, nobody told Bigfoot!

This is a picture of the Wills Creek, Ohio area where
Tyler had his encounter with something terrifying on
his 2012 hunting trip.

Tyler made the three and a half hour trip from his hometown of Hamilton, Ohio to the Wills Creek Reservoir alone as his hunting partner had to back out at the last minute. He was so stoked at the idea of bagging one of these antlered giants that he didn't seem to mind being alone. After all, he had hunted alone many times before. It wouldn't be any big deal at all. He reached the area on Thursday morning. A week before Thanksgiving he stopped at the Wills Creek General Store and talked to the owner, Tammy. He asked several questions about the area, as this was his first trip there. He got his necessary permits and set off to drive around and explore the region. He drove out County Road 410 which runs right along Wills Creek for a ways until either the road turns or the creek turns or both turn and you can't see one from the other anymore. He smiled as he took notice of the remoteness of the place. You could drive for a long way without seeing any houses, just woods, fields and every now and then he could see the creek to his right and he decided that this is where he would pitch his tent and hunt for the next four days. He would have the place to himself. . . he thought! He turned his truck around with his 14 foot boat and trailer following obediently behind. He made his way back down County Road 410 to the Wills Creek boat ramp. He loaded all his gear from the truck into the boat and backed down the ramp into the muddy water below. The boat slid off easily as the lake was up due to recent fall rains. He parked his truck and climbed aboard and with a choke and 2 pulls on the rope, the Evinrude roared to life. He pointed the vessel upstream toward the logjam, towards Plainfield, one of the Squatchiest places in Ohio. There have been tons of sightings and encounters in this area of Ohio but little did Tyler know about this. Tyler didn't even really believe in Bigfoot, no, he was there for the whitetail deer and a big one, too, one to hang on the wall and admire and tell all his friends about. Yes, this would be a great trip and a great hunt and he was just as excited as a kid at Christmas to have this awesome place to himself. He traveled maybe a mile by water until he found a place where he could pull his boat up into another little creek that fed into Wills Creek. He unloaded his tent and all his gear and set up his camp right by the water. This was perfect he thought. He could see the creek but the road, County Road 410 was out of sight of where his camp would be. He gathered firewood but later decided against having a campfire that way if someone drove down the road that night they couldn't see his fire flickering through the trees. He did get in his tree stand and hunt for a while but saw no deer although he did hear two bucks fighting. It sounded like they were on the other side of the creek. Ok, Tyler thought, that's what I'm here for. But as dusk settled in he descended the tree and said to himself, that's fine, I've got three more days to get Mr. Big. Tyler ate a sandwich for supper and deciding not to have a campfire so he got into his tent and lit one of his emergency camp heat containers. He read for a while and finally shut off his lantern and fell asleep zipped up inside his nylon abode. It was around midnight or a little after when he awoke and was aware of the fact that he was cold. His heat source had gone out. He unzipped his sleeping bag and was in the process of lighting another heat container when from somewhere outside his tent, in the darkness, there came a terrifying scream some 20 seconds long that tapered off into a growl. A multitude of thoughts raced through Tyler's brain, one of which was that he was going to be killed out there by something that he had never encountered before. Tyler unzipped his tent and stepped out into the foggy blackness, a knife in one hand and a light in the other trying to penetrate the mist that had surrounded the whole valley. He screamed back at the midnight visitor who he could hear stomping off in the distance on what must have been two legs. Tyler dove for his crossbow and nocked an arrow in and again weighed his chances of making it out of there alive. He snapped a few pictures of his camp with his phone camera in the event that something did rip him to pieces and carry him off and eat him. Maybe someone would find his phone and see a picture of what killed him. He decided that his only chance of survival was to break camp and so break camp he did. Bending and breaking the tent poles, he grabbed everything that he had brought with him in mere seconds and threw the whole lot into his boat and shoving off into the foggy waterway. Tyler's heart was pounding like a Gene Krupa solo. Thank God his faithful

Evinrude started right up like a real trooper and thank God he had a spotlight on the boat so he could find his way back in these horrible traveling conditions. His mind raced as he inched his way back to the ramp all the while expecting the thing to come after him. What was it? Bigfoot maybe, but no, he didn't believe in Bigfoot. He had even made fun of the mere thought of Bigfoot before but now he wasn't so sure about it. He didn't know what else could have been as loud as that scream was. So bloodcurdling, yes, he thought, that must be it, that had to be what he heard, Bigfoot was real! He scanned the muddy water ahead of the boat hoping that the thing wouldn't come after him. Thinking about his wife and kids, would he make it out alive? Would he ever see them again? Finally after what seemed like a lifetime, Tyler saw the light from the boat ramp up ahead and started to feel a little better. He loaded his boat in record time all the while his head doing owl turns in all directions looking for the midnight screamer until finally the rig was road worthy. He left the area in a rush and headed west to Coshocton, where he was able to secure a motel room for the night. Finally, receiving a signal, his cell phone was working so he called his wife at 3:30 a.m. and still shaking in his shoes Tyler told her what had happened to him and that he was ok and everything was fine now and that he now believed in Bigfoot!

Here's the picture Tyler took with his cellphone of his tent and campsite in the fog thinking that if he were killed that night, someone would find his phone and see his pictures and piece together the story of his demise.

Butt Print

In June 2009, I got an urgent call from my friend Chris. He was working out of state and he had received a text message from his daughter just minutes before. She and a friend had been hiking in the woods and fields behind their Pleasant City home. They found an area on a hilltop south of town where it appeared that something big sat down to watch the houses down below. There was a huge butt print and footprints in the tall grass and other footprints, large ones that had flattened the grass. The girls sniffed at the flattened area and reported a very pungent and offensive odor. There was a small patch of woods some 25 yards away from the girls and while checking out the area and taking photos, they both heard a growl come from this small woodlot. This frightened the two kids and they ran for the safety of their homes down below in town. I went back out to the area the next day with Chris' daughter, Ali. She was nervous at the thought of going back to the place after having been scared off just one day before but since I was with her she felt safe. I guess that's because in a foot race for safety, I would have been the one caught and gobbled up by an angry Bigfoot! The tracks and flattened areas of where something sat down were still plainly evident but I was unable to detect an odor coming from the spot nor any hair of any kind. I sat in the exact spot and could see where his feet had smashed down the grass some 2½ feet in front of the butt print. Something had sat there and watched the yards and houses down below. I wondered if they had children that played in the yard or maybe the man or woman that lived there had been cutting the grass or working in the yard. Anyway, it was a perfect vantage point for the big guy to just sit and watch the people down below. We didn't find any more evidence and since the heat and humidity were both very uncomfortable, we left after about an hour. There have been sightings in this area before. Dreama Elkins was featured on the Ohio segment of the History channel's MonsterQuest. She awakened late at night and saw one in the yard possibly looking in her window. If her barking dog hadn't awakened her, she might not have ever known that it was out there. We continue to get reports of activity from the Pleasant City area to this very day.

Was a Bigfoot sitting here in the grass watching the houses in Pleasant City, Ohio?

You can see where the feet were mashed into the grass. Sitting here would provide a great view of the scenery.

Batesville Investigation

Another investigation that we went to check out occurred near the intersection of Guernsey, Belmont and Monroe Counties, not too far from Batesville. It happened during the summer of 2011. It was a very hot time of year with temps reaching the mid 90's frequently. A friend of mine, who incidentally had a Bigfoot encounter of her own, called me one day and told me of a co-worker who was having some strange things going on around her home. We talked on the phone and made plans to see her the next evening. Judy, Shawna and I met with her and her daughter and son-in-law at their home and listened to their story as we sat around the kitchen table. The couple had a new baby and the father smoked so he would go out on the front porch to light up. He began hearing brush breaking and growling noises from the wooded area across the road from the house at night whenever he sat on the porch. He had his wife and mother-in-law both come outside to listen, too, and both verified that they had heard it also. He stated that one time he was out on the porch late at night talking to a friend in another state on his cellphone. He said that the growls and tree snaps were so loud that his friend on the phone asked him what was going on. He couldn't hear him talking for all the commotion. They also told us that they had found a Bigfoot track in the backyard and that something had pounded on the back of the house late at night. We learned that they had been throwing garbage and food scraps out behind the house. Also, the baby was another possible attraction for Bigfoot. When they learned that the creatures have a fascination for children and especially babies, they put the little one in a different bedroom. I explained to the mother how on more than one occasion, a Bigfoot had been seen looking in children's bedroom windows. Upon hearing this they changed the baby's room to an interior one without any windows. They also stopped putting out table scraps. Four SOSBI members went to the location and stayed until the wee hours of the morning looking for signs and listening for any sounds of the hairy critters. As it happens sometimes, nothing was found and nothing happened. After a week or so of the aforementioned incidents, all activity stopped. I saw the son-in-law in town a few months later and he told me that there had been no more activity at their residence.

Hunters Become the Hunted

Another fellow, Mark, contacted SOSBI about an encounter that he and three other men had while bow hunting in rural Belmont County not far from where the couple with the baby lived with her mother near the town of Batesville. The men arrived in the wee hours of the morning and parked along a gravel road. As soon as the quartet exited their vehicles they began hearing the sounds of a Barred Owl up in the woods, who cooks who cooks for you? It was soon joined by a second Barred Owl and the two bantered back and forth while the hunters climbed the hill in the direction of the area that they had planned to hunt. By this time the hunters had become suspicious of the owl sounds and Mark said that although the sounds were very similar to that of a Barred Owl, they just didn't quite sound right. Bigfoot have been known to mimic a large array of birds and animals, humans included and sometimes they don't quite get it right! They also began to hear twigs and sticks snapping that sounded like two individuals were stalking the men somewhere in the darkness behind them. Every time the men would stop to listen for the sounds of someone following them, the pair of pursuers would also come to a stop. This is thought to be a classic Bigfoot maneuver used while stalking people. Mark even held back and let the other three men proceed, only to hear the two creatures following behind start up again thinking that they all had started moving again. After about a half hour of this cat and mouse game, the four arrived at a small plateau and took a break to rest for a while. After a few minutes, the darkened silence was shattered with a thunderous scream that sent shivers up and down the spines of the hunters. The hair on their arms and backs of their necks was standing at full attention. They gripped their bows in anticipation of an attack of some sort only none came, just silence except for their own rapid breathing and the pounding of their hearts in their chests. They formed a tight cluster and tried to see into the inky blackness of the predawn morning. The tiny flashlights that they carried made a feeble attempt to illuminate the source of the scream that just seconds earlier had sent their blood pressure to the danger point. One man had had enough! He wanted to try and make a run for it back down the hill to the safety of his pickup, parked on the roadside below. Mark took charge of the situation and said, "No!" There were four of them and they all had bows and arrows nocked. They had come all the way from Akron to hunt deer and that's what they were going to do! After several tense moments with no more screams, the foursome continued on as planned further up the hill until they came to an area that they had wanted to hunt. Instead of stringing out in a line a hundred yards apart, each hunter selected a tree within sight of another man and climbed up and sat in wait of deer that never did come. Mark said that the woods were overwhelming with an eerie silence. They never did hear whatever screamed walk away or make another sound. It was sometime before the woods returned to normal and they started seeing and hearing birds and squirrels and all the normal noises that a hunter experiences while enjoying his sport. Deer hunting will never be the same for the men on this hunt; it never is for someone who has experienced the presence of a Sasquatch.

Grand Haven Resort Sighting

SOSBI was invited to participate in a Bigfoot themed weekend at Grand Haven Resorts, which is just northwest of Salt Fork State Park, during August 2011. An employee of the 850 plus acre resort had been to a few of our meetings and was convinced that there was a Bigfoot presence there. He was their Naturalist and was in the woods conducting nature walks, night hikes and such and had experienced some Bigfoot behavior for a while, such as tree breaks, screams and such. A handful of us went out and setup a display for their members and guests to examine and while there I was approached by a retired minister from Central Ohio who I will call John. John and his wife have a camper at Grand Haven where they can come and go as they please and enjoy the amenities. John took me and Dave, another SOSBI member over to his place on his golf cart. He had found tracks in his backyard where a Bigfoot had come up out of the woods from a very steep ravine behind his trailer. It appeared that a birdfeeder filled with sunflower seeds was what had attracted the beast as it had been emptied by something during the night. Raccoons would be the normal suspects except they don't leave 20 inch long by 8 inch wide tracks on the ground like we found there. I got a phone call from John about a week later and went back out to meet him as he said that his wife had actually seen the creature in the tree line as they sat at a picnic table in the backyard talking. John had his back to the trees but his wife was able to catch a glimpse of a black figure in the trees watching them for a few seconds. They had been awakened the night before by a horrible smell that invaded their camper bedroom and caused them to pull the covers over their heads to try to escape the intrusive odor. John checked the yard later in the morning and found more tracks close to their bedroom where it had walked by. The creature was careful to step on flat rocks in the yard so as not to leave tracks but we were able to find two. We took pictures and cast one footprint that was 20" by 8" again. Our same boy as before it appears! John later learned from a neighbor just down the road that he had seen deer and other quadrupeds coming up and out of the wooded ravine behind John's side of the road and cross to the woods on the other side of the road. It was a kind of animal exodus, if you will. That must have been when our big boy moved into the deep ravine behind John's place. The neighbor also stated that he couldn't get his dogs to go outside for potty breaks anymore. He had to drag them out and they appeared afraid and wanted to immediately be let back inside! They had never shown this type of behavior until now. Something was different. The SOSBI crew did calls late that night and played a recording of the Sierra Sounds into the woods by the shooting range. They got lots of audible responses back and saw eyeshine coming from the woods but no actual sighting that could be claimed to be a Bigfoot was made. I continue to this day to call John to see if any more activity has happened and if and when it does, we will go back out and see what we can find.

After casting the 19" to 20" footprint found at Grand Haven, we snapped this picture.

Janet's Sighting

While at Grand Haven, one of the guests of a member came to our display table and told us of a sighting that she had experienced the year before at Burr Oak State Park. Her name is Janet Minger, and she and her son and her brother been camping at Burr Oak and were hiking on what is known as the Lakeview Trail. Quite a distance from where they had pitched their tent, Janet's son left the trail that they had been on and took a different route in search of arrowheads or something. As the adults caught up with him, Janet's brother noticed some kind of tree structure down the hill a ways and walked over to it for a closer look. Summoning Janet and her son over to inspect the find, the trio was perplexed to discover that this was some sort of a hunting blind. It had all sorts of brush and sticks and limbs and they were all woven together like a basket she told me. It wasn't a natural wind damaged brush pile. No, someone or something with hands had carefully placed each limb and branch to its liking and intertwined them in a manner to offer strength as well as concealment for whomever or whatever hid inside and watched the game trail nearby. Why would a person make such an apparatus they questioned as they looked around some more? They also remembered that this was in a part of the park that wasn't even supposed to allow hunting and this structure would take much too long for a person to build anyway. You can buy tent-like, camo-colored ground blinds and they aren't very expensive either. Janet was beginning to feel uneasy at this point, thinking that something other than men had made this structure and started looking around up ahead and down below where they stood. She had a monocular in her pocket and carefully checked the surrounding area when suddenly she was shocked to see a dark figure hiding amongst the trees down below them observing them. The figure quickly disappeared behind a tree and her heart rate shot up and Janet exclaimed, "Something is down below us and it's watching us." She tried to describe to her brother which tree the figure was hiding behind when she saw it peek around again and then duck back through the lens of the monocular. Just then Janet was astounded to see a hairy arm and hairy human-shaped hand with fingers reach around from behind the backside of the tree and grasp the trunk of the tree and hold on! "We have to leave, now!" Janet cried out as she pushed her son ahead of her and bolted back up the hill to the trail. They beat a hasty retreat all the way back to where they had pitched their tent. Without further incident until a year later when they would return and have yet another encounter with the hairy-handed ground blind builder of Burr Oak State Park.

Gayle's Stalking

A lady named Gayle attended one of our meetings and spoke with me during the break. It turns out that we went to high school together. She had been watching the Finding Bigfoot program for a while and had become very interested in the subject. She studied the map that I had made and took a few notes of area inside Salt Fork State Park where there had been several incidents of humans coming into contact with Bigfoot. Deciding on the area of the Kennedy Stone House Trail, she, her son and her little dog drove out to the park not long after the meeting day and walked the almost 2 mile path from the parking lot to the Stone House. Along the way they tried some tree knocks and some of the howls and screams that the cast members of Finding Bigfoot do on the program. When they reached the Stone House, they discovered that there were other people there so they decided to wait until the others left and then they would try some more of the screams and howls. As the sun was nearing the Western horizon, the other people had all left and Gayle and her son resumed the calls into the evening air. She said she thought they heard a scream come back from somewhere up in the woods but she wasn't sure from what. Something caught her attention though that gave her pause for concern, far off to the west in the dark evening sky she could see lighting which indicated a storm was coming in. Knowing that they had almost 2 miles to walk to get to the car, they left and proceeded along the path towards the parking lot. By this time it was quite dark and they had flashlights but something else was amiss now. Her little dog which had been quite happy earlier in the hike, running ahead and sniffing butterflies and enjoying the outing was now whimpering and whining and trying to stay right under Gayle's feet. It kept looking back behind them on the trail and they began to hear something stalking them from behind and slightly up the hill from them. They would stop and shine their lights back behind them and up into the trees and rocks, but they couldn't see what it was. It knew that they were trying to listen to it because every time they stopped to listen it would stop, too. It was like a game but it was very unnerving to them. At one spot when they stopped to listen, large rocks came hurtling out of the woods above them splashing into the lake to their left. From the sounds of the splashing the rock had to be large! This really caused the frightened hikers to hasten their exodus from the woods causing Gayle to become overheated. She peeled off her sweater she wore as she hurried along the trail flipping off a brand new pair of glasses somewhere into the vegetation along the path. Gayle has still not recovered her glasses to this day. But did all this frightening activity dissuade Gayle and her son from further Bigfoot excursions? Not at all, because this just seemed to wet their appetite. They often go out at night and make a fire and sit and do calls and wait for a response. I have shared company with them on a few occasions myself, sitting around a campfire or hiking the hills and valleys of Salt Fork in pursuit of evidence of our quest.

The Paul Hayes' Encounter

We were contacted in the fall of 2011 by a man named Paul Hayes, who lives south of Akron not too far from Minerva. Minerva is the sight of some famous Bigfoot activity that took place in the 70's and 80's that made national news and had hundreds of people, some of them armed to the teeth, come to hunt down the monster! I talked to a couple of the witnesses recently and they were very unhappy and disgusted with the way strangers trampled across their land, trespassed in their yards and blocked their driveways with their own vehicles in a fevered riot to find the creature and kill it to prove that it was real. Hopefully, we are all past that point now. It was really a hotbed of activity back in the day. Paul doesn't live too far from where all this took place and what he told me sounds like he, too, has one or at least had one staying behind his house. This was confirmed according to Paul when he and his son saw it standing by a tree watching them look for any signs of it having been there. Paul said it kind of swayed back and forth as if it would shift its massive weight from one leg to the other. It all started when Paul was having a smoke on his back porch one night and he heard something growling from out in the tree line in the darkness. It happened the next night, too. His wife confirmed that she too had heard growling coming from out back behind the house whenever she stood on the back porch at night. Paul and his cousin, Chris, went out in the woods one day below the house to look around for some clues as to what this growling creature could be. They found various tree structures, a track, some human looking scat that was buried with leaves in a field of picked corn and most interesting was an igloo type structure that someone or something had made by a game trail in the woods. Chris entered the structure that was made by weaving together brush, limbs, grass, leaves, etc. Chris stated that it must have been 10 feet deep inside of the structure. Unfortunately, they didn't take any pictures or video of the igloo structure and when they returned a week later to do just that, the structure was gone. Not just torn down, mind you, but completely gone including the materials from which it was made. Paul's theory is that the Bigfoot either saw Chris enter the structure or smelled that he had been in it so it tore its own shelter down and left the area. Other suspicious happenings around Paul's house included smelling a horrible stinky smell outside at night that was very strong even inside the garage, leaving one to wonder if it had been inside the garage since the door had been open. Probably the most convincing to me was hearing that one night Paul saw two large orange eyes illuminated in the darkness. He said that they were up high, way off the ground. When Paul opened up the back door, his little house dog took off like a shot straight towards the orange eyes, yapping all the way. As the dog disappeared into the darkness, Paul saw the eyes blink and move in what had to have been orange eyes turning its head to look at the barking canine. The yapping of the dog suddenly changed into a yelping, yippy, hurt, scared sound. The pooch was somehow able to reverse course and scoot back into the porch and inside the house to safety. I told Paul that he was lucky to get his pet back alive considering Bigfoot's poor track record when it comes to getting along with barking dogs. Five of us from SOSBI spent the better part of a day at Paul's location looking around. We didn't see a Bigfoot but we did see some strange tree breaks and formations in the woods below his house. Paul was transformed from a worried resident of an area with some Squatch activity into a full time Bigfoot believer, researcher, blogger, and investigator. He spends most of his free time researching these giants either online or in the woods.

"I almost hit it". . .

One October evening in 2011 right around dusk, Berlin Center resident, Sally Palumbo, was driving on Western Reserve Road in Mahoning County. Turning left onto Stratton Road, Sally was shocked to see a 7 foot tall and 3 to 4 foot wide dark brown hairy creature suddenly appear before her vehicle in its jaunt across the road from one wooded area to an open field before disappearing into the woods east of Route 45. She estimates the whole incident was over 10 to 15 seconds. Sally told me that she almost drove into the ditch as she continued making a left turn in her moving car as her unbelieving eyes were locked on the hairy ape-man. She said she was so terrified that she abandoned her original destination of Salem and returned home. Still shaken she woke her husband and told him what she had seen. It had very long hair on its arms that she could see very plainly as it crossed in front of her car. Sally did a little detective work and found out that a neighbor had a sighting the year before in an area very close to this. In checking my maps I discovered that Minerva is only 20 miles or so away from where her sighting took place. That is 20 miles as the crow flies or the Bigfoot strides, which is not that far in that case. Also, Lisbon to the south of this has had some sightings reported lately. Several members of the Ohio Bigfoot Hunters have found evidence in this part of the state as well. It's important to really pay attention when traveling to this area as you may be the next to see something that you might not be sure existed!

Bigfoot Magnets

Some people search for years or a whole lifetime for the legendary Bigfoot creature without ever seeing one. Sometimes they may hear their cries at night or maybe discover a track or two in the mud but an actual encounter or sighting never happens to them. Others, however, it seems are Bigfoot magnets if you will. I'm not talking about a habituation situation where the resident Bigfoot family gets used to the property owners or residents of the house on the grounds. In that scenario, the humans gain the trust of the Bigfoot and eventually they will begin to be seen much more easily. They are not nearly as apt to remain hidden whenever the humans are around. Sometimes they even allow the humans the opportunity to observe them in the daylight and view their young as well. It usually takes months if not years to gain their trust before this happens. The humans leave gifts of fruit, meat, toys, etc., that the Squatches take with them. In return, Bigfoot often leave something in return for their human friends which may be a rock, stick or an animal carcass of something they killed and gifted back to the humans! No, I'm talking about Bigfoot magnets, people such as Lorena Cunningham and Janet Minger who have had encounters more than once in different locations and none of these encounters occurred where they lived. In the case of Lorena, her second encounter occurred in 2004 just a few weeks before her third incident (the barn encounter). Lorena's mother had died and she went to stay with her elderly father who was in the beginning stages of Alzheimer's. They stayed in her childhood home a few miles down the road from her current home in Nobel County. The old house was kept company on the grounds by a barn, a garage and a few other sheds and outbuildings. There were horses on the farm kept in place by a barbed wire fence and gates here and there. One cold January day in 2004, Lorena's daughter and her fiancé came to visit Lorena and her dad. When their visit was over Lorena told her daughter and fiancé that when they drove away they didn't need to get back out of the car to shut the gate because she would come out of the house herself and close it. Minutes after their departure, true to her word, Lorena went out the back door of the house to secure the gate. She was standing by the corner of the house when to her surprise she saw a very tall man in a grey coat walking along the fence headed towards the barn. Lorena couldn't understand what in the world some man would be doing on their property in the winter, especially since he seemed to have come from up in the woods and not from below the house towards the road. It was only when this very tall man in the grey coat got closer and passed beside several 8 foot corner posts that were bundled up and leaning against the fence that she realized that he was a good foot taller than the posts. Next, came the realization that the grey coat on the man was not a coat at all but grey hair. She thought this thing was looking at the ground in an attempt to watch its footing so as not to slip on the ice and snow of this Ohio winter day. She realized then that this thing was going to come within mere feet of where she was standing by the house on its way to the warmth of the hay filled barn. Her mind raced back to that day 20 years before with her kids at the playground. "Oh, my God!" she thought, "Not again!" but something was different this time. Lorena observed that this creature was much taller and lanky, kind of old looking with grey hair and all. Lorena told me she thought that the creature was probably watching the ground and failed to see her was because it didn't want to fall or maybe it had arthritis or something. Later, Lorena said that some Bigfoot Researchers told her that the Bigfoot was probably carefully watching where it walked to avoid leaving tracks for anyone to find. The Bigfoot Lorena had seen with her kids in

1984 was a female with breasts clearly visible. It was darker in color, too, and 7 to 7½ feet tall and very wide. This was a different creature entirely. Regardless of the sex of the beast, she didn't want it coming any closer to her on its way to the barn. She struggled to find her voice and finally blurted out, "Hey!" she barely choked out and then she found her voice, "Hey, what do you think you're doing?" The giant jerked his head up with its mouth open in surprise to return Lorena's wide-eyed stare and it froze momentarily before twisting around and reversing direction and quickly walking back in the direction it had come from until it disappeared from sight up into the woods above the house. In its haste to leave, it left 20 inch tracks behind. A chill ran up Lorena's spine partly from the encounter and partly from the cold Ohio weather. She quickly returned to the inside of the house to find her father standing by the window. Lorena was worried that the old fella had witnessed the intruder and would be alarmed and afraid of what he had to have seen take place just a few yards away outside until he announced to his daughter as only a parent can do, "You forgot to shut the gate." He never mentioned the creature to her.

This is a picture of where the tall grey Bigfoot was walking along the fence line when Lorena spotted it. In the middle behind the fence you can see the 8 foot fence posts stacked up and the creature was at least a foot taller than these posts.

Hollywood Calls

My cellphone rang on the afternoon of July 20, 2011, and I was in line at the bank drive-through and noticed that the number was one that I didn't recognize. It was from area code 818. . .hmmm. . .probably someone wanting to know when the next Bigfoot meeting was. I answered just as the teller inside the bank decided to talk to me on the intercom. "Let me call you right back." I told the phone caller. Little did I realize that I'd just hung up on Hollywood. Five minutes later when I called the number back I was very surprised to find out that I was talking to Natalie Hewson of Ping Pong Productions. She was a producer for the Finding Bigfoot program on the Animal Planet channel. She told me that she had found my name and number on the internet on the SOSBI page and was enlisting my help in lining up a meeting place for the town hall meeting for the cast of the television show this coming September for the Ohio segments. She also wanted me to help her with contacting or locating people who had seen a Bigfoot or had some kind of encounter with one. Wow! This was so awesome. Natalie and I texted and talked several times over the next few months and although they didn't choose to have the meeting in the location I found for them, the one they got was even better. The Deerassic Park meeting room was packed to the rafters when 3 of the 4 cast members (Bobo was solo camping at Salt Fork) walked in the side door and marched up in front of 175 Bigfoot aficionados. Several people, including me, got to stand up and tell Matt, Cliff and Ranae about sightings, sounds, track finds and just about anything you can think of Bigfoot related for the next two hours. Several SOSBI people spoke and Lorena was even featured on the show. They did a re-enactment of her sighting with the kids at the Sharon Grange playground. Now remember Janet from the Burr Oak sighting? Well, her story intrigued Matt Moneymaker so he wanted to meet with her and her brother in a few days back down in Morgan County and see where her sighting took place the year before. She was worried that they wouldn't be able to find the exact same spot where this happened because they had never been back there since it took place. They decided to go back down the day before they were to meet the T.V. crew just so they wouldn't embarrass everyone if they couldn't remember. They parked the car and the pair hit the trail and was soon closing in on the area of the sighting. They were telling each other little things that were coming back to them as they hiked nearer and nearer to the spot when out of nowhere came a thud as a rock came hurtling out of the woods and landed on the bank beside them. Now for those of you who may not know this, Bigfoot throws rocks. If you get near a Bigfoot and it feels you are coming too close, it can and will do one of several things. One of which is to throw a rock at you or several rocks, big ones sometimes to get your attention and give you second thoughts about proceeding any further. So either Ernest T. Bass was in the woods that day throwing rocks at windows or the Bigfoot from the year before still wanted to be left alone. I am betting it was a Bigfoot.

When they returned the following day with Matt and the T.V. crew, the rock was still laying there but no sign of the Bigfoot was seen. Four of us went back later on and checked it out again with no further incidents. But the experience with the cast and crew members of the show was a positive one and I felt honored to have assisted anyway I could in the making of the Ohio episode of the cast members and found them to be very respectful and supportive of our efforts at SOSBI.

Author, Doug Waller poses here with Bobo Fay from the Animal Planet series, Finding Bigfoot.

Janet's Third Encounter

Hosak's Cave sign warning hikers not to proceed to the top of the cave after 4 people have fallen and 2 of those have died.

If you exit Route 22 and get on Road 1 inside Salt Fork State Park and drive about a quarter of a mile, you will see a parking lot and building on your right. This is the Park Information Office. One may obtain information of the various amenities the park has to offer or get maps and brochures, or use the rest rooms. Janet Minger is thankful for the restrooms! No, it's not what you think; she didn't eat a bad burrito from the lodge or anything like that. She had to hide in the restroom from something outside in the darkness that knew she was inside.

Let's start at the beginning. Janet and her son, and her brother, Edward and his son, drove from their Reynoldsburg area home to Salt Fork to do some hiking and exploring after several hours of enjoying the different trails that the park has to offer. The group was finishing up on their last hike of the day, in the Hosak Cave area. When the hikers returned to the parking lot just before dusk it was only then that they discovered that they had lost the car keys. With darkness closing in and their only flashlight locked inside the car, there was no way to hunt for the lost keys. Janet's cellphone was rendered useless due to the notorious dead spot that the parking lot at the cave area is famous for as far as cellphones go. Yes, they were in a real pickle. After some time there appeared a set of headlights approaching from the main road. As they squinted at the oncoming vehicle as it drew closer a welcome sight became visible on the door of the truck, *PARK RANGER*. Janet quickly approached the truck as the driver's window went down. She explained their dilemma to the female officer inside. The lady ranger told them to get in and she would take them back to the park office where her cellphone should work just fine, plenty of signal there. Besides the parking lot of Hosak's Cave wasn't a safe place the ranger said, "I don't like this place. Too many strange things go on here!" She explained that she was assigned to another state park and that she was just filling in for a local ranger who was on vacation, "I just hate it whenever I have to come up here to work." The ranger said that she had heard the stories of the Sasquatches here and other unexplained things as well. Even she had seen creatures along the road at night that she thought might have been the legendary beasts. She had to make two trips to get the four people delivered to the information office lot and after making sure that Janet's cellphone could make a call from this location, left them to go on patrol. The ranger assured them that she would return again later to check on them. Her truck disappeared into the night as Janet pushed the home button on her phone and waited for her husband to answer. Although the office was closed and locked up, there were inside restrooms available to them and an outside light was on in the parking lot, plus Janet had cell service here. Just then her husband's voice was heard as he answered her call. She explained the situation and assured him that they were all fine but he needed to drive to Salt Fork to pick them up and other arrangements would be made later to retrieve Ed's car from the parking lot at the cave. As the group settled in for a two hour wait, they first sat at the picnic table for a while and talked. Tiring of this after a while they walked out into the parking lot and scanned the night sky looking for shooting stars and constellations. It was a beautiful clear autumn night in September and the black world overhead was alive with countless twinkling stars and planets and the group was mesmerized. We don't get to see the night sky like this very often, Janet told me, too many lights from the city and that ruins it. As a matter of fact, facing south, as they were, the only light she remembers seeing at all was to her left to the east. "It was causing a glare in my glasses, so I put my left hand up to block the light from my eyes." Janet told me. It had to be from the Salt Fork State Park sign out at Route 22. She said that they continued to watch the sky for a long time and every time she put her hand down she said that that darned light would bother her. At some point, Janet noticed that the glare to her left was gone, as if the light had gone out. She began looking to her left where the light had been and she was able to see a huge hulking shape standing in the shadows between them and the light and it seemed to be watching them. She tore her brother's attention away from the sky and pointed to the thing and commanded him to look in the direction where she was pointing. Her brother tried to focus where she had told him to look and simultaneously they both saw it move closer towards them. All hell broke loose as the brother and sister each grabbed their sons and pushed them into a run for the safety of the restroom. As the four piled into the women's room, one of the boys tried to retrieve their belongings off of the picnic table. "Leave it!" Janet shouted as she slammed the door behind her and locked it. They scarcely breathed as they listened for the beast lurking outside the door. After a few tense moments, the group was again terrified even further when they started hearing very heavy bipedal stomping outside and even felt the floor they were sitting on moving from the massively weighted creature just outside the door. When it moved, the floor would sag, just as the hayloft floor did that day over Lorena's head. A guttural grunt was heard just outside and the creature stopped its movement and stood still for a few minutes. Janet remembered that their things were still on the picnic table outside and thought perhaps it was inspecting the items. After a moment, the floor moved again as the lumbering giant ambled away into the night. She tried calling her husband again but the cellphone wouldn't work nearly as well inside the bathroom as it had worked outside in the parking lot. "Well, that's out." she said. She was not leaving that room until her husband got there. Finally, after several attempts, she reached Gene on the phone and learned that he wasn't very far away. A short while later they could hear a horn honking and then her phone rang. It was Gene and he was outside in the parking lot and he was calling to ask where they were. They slowly opened the door and peeked out. Seeing nothing resembling the Hairy Man Beast, the group made a mad dash to the safety of Gene's car and headed for home.

Final Thoughts from the Author

SOSBI continues to bring researcher and witnesses together so that we can learn more and more about Bigfoot and try to understand just what they are and who they are. Are they people? Do they have rights like we do? What lies ahead for them in the future? Can we continue to co-exist? That depends entirely on us. They have survived all this time without our intervention and it's my belief that it's in their best interest to continue that way.

Broken/arched trees in Salt Fork State Park, Ohio
These are found in areas of Bigfoot activity and are thought
by Bigfoot Researchers to be a type of sign made by Bigfoot.

Broken trees as in the picture above are also thought by researchers to be a form of communication by Bigfoot in areas of Bigfoot activity. This picture was taken in Salt Fork State Park.

Another picture taken in Salt Fork State Park, these are called pinwheel structures by some Bigfoot researchers. It is unknown what their meaning is but thought to be form of communication by Bigfoot. These are found all over North America in areas of Bigfoot activity.

Hosak's Cave in Salt Fork State Park, Ohio where there have been reports of Bigfoot. Visitors are not allowed any closer to the cave since 2 people have fallen to their deaths from atop the cave area.

This is a picture of the author contemplating where to look next for Bigfoot in Salt Fork State Park.

Bridge over the creek near Hosak's Cave in Salt Fork State Park where there has reportedly been a lot of Bigfoot activity.

Footprint cast by Donna Wells Fink and Jackie Riesterer of the SWWO Southern Wisconsin's Wild Ones in Salt Fork State Park in 2012 near the Primitive Campground area after a report was given to the author a few days prior of a Bigfoot sighting. Note the mid-tarsal break in the footprint.

Mark and Jeanne Hudak at a SOSBI campout in Salt Fork State Park.

A huge structure thought to have been built by Bigfoot in Salt Fork State Park.

SOSBI member, Shawna Parks is pictured here with Ranae Holland of Animal Planet's Finding Bigfoot.

Water falls near Hosak's Cave in Salt Fork State Park.

A bowed tree structure in Salt Fork State Park. Note how the top of the tree is held down by other objects. These structures are thought to be a form of Bigfoot communication also.

SOSBI's logo.

SOSBI map of Guernsey County with a close-up of the Salt Fork State Park, Ohio area.

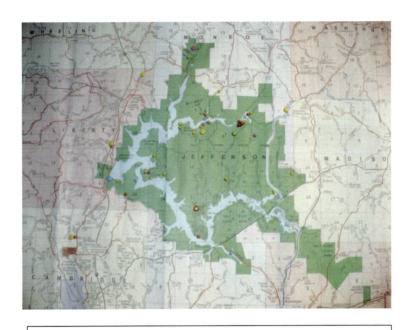

SOSBI map where pins of different colors note sightings, tracks, vocalizations, stalkings, etc., in the Salt Fork State Park area.

The author, Doug Waller is pictured here with Bobo Faye of Animal Planet's Finding Bigfoot show.

Morgan's Knob Loop Trail at Salt Fork State Park where there have been reports of Bigfoot activity.

The author, Doug Waller poses here in Salt Fork State Park, Ohio.